The Beacon

Spring 2018

9th Edition

Editor in Chief

Laura A. Lord

Faculty Advisors

Dave Harper

Interim Vice President Workforce and Academic Programs

Linda Earls

Associate Professor of English

Contributors

Artwork and Photography

Graham Alston - *Corvid*

Josh Anderson – *Slowly Drifting, Spiraling Out of Control*, and *Success is a Staircase, not a Doorway*

Melissa Comfort – *Alcatraz* and *Shocked*

Rachael Kamm – *Thomas Point Lighthouse, Maryland's State Flower*, and *Sandy Point Lighthouse*

Miriam Moran - *Fusion*

Vinny Parreco – *Chesapeake Sunset, Love in a Lens*, and *Dragonfly*

Poetry

Alanah Filion – *Beauty, Death and Decay* and *The Cage*

Dianna Greene - *Waiting*

Laura A. Lord – *Blue Bird* and *Noise Machine*

Marissa Moldoch – *Beach Day*

Rebekkah Napier - *Hurt*

Jacky Smith – *Epiphany, Please Not Me*, and *Youth*

Prose

Katondra Cherry-Jenkins – *Home, Sweet Home*

Rob Dey – *Margarite*

Debra Jones – *A Twisted Turn*

Laura A. Lord – *Sin-Eater*

Marissa Moldoch – *Finding My Passion*

Kendall M. Pearl – *The Fall of a Flower*

Plays & Scenes

E. C. Collins – *The Coma*

Jacky Smith – *Six Sisters*

Chesapeake Sunset

Photographer: Vinny Parreco

Vinny Parreco is a Chesapeake College Alumni, Class of 2017. He writes, "Beautiful landscapes exist in all forms throughout this magnificent planet, but none compare to the sight that many on Maryland's Eastern Shore are lucky to call home."

Table of Contents

Alcatraz

Photographer: Melissa Comfort

Melissa Comfort is a current student at Chesapeake College. She is a 17-year-old, dual-enrollment senior from Queen Anne's Country High School. Her favorite type of photography is film and she's been shooting photography for a little over four years. She hopes to become a professional photographer in the future.

Cover Art

Epiphany
By Jacky Smith

It was easy to call him a monster,
he certainly looked the part -
crashing fists, thunderous roars, gnashing teeth.
And he bit.
And bit again.
And you did nothing.
Even then, I knew that you held the leash.
You invited him in,
your pet.
You pointed at him, the monster,
while you, with surgical precision,
laid the jagged shards of
self-doubt and self-loathing in me.
And now, you're gone.
Here I stand - a bleeding patchwork of pain.
I will not honor tradition and pass those shards down.
Sinking in a bottomless pit of rage with
no place to aim the pain, but at myself.
Drowning in your monstrous love.

Jacky Smith is a first-year student at Chesapeake College. She is married and is the mother to a son and daughter. She particularly enjoys immersing herself in books.

Success is a Staircase, not a Doorway

Photographer: Josh Anderson

Josh Anderson is a full-time student at Chesapeake College. He is majoring in business administration, with hopes to transfer after two years. With his degree in business, Josh hopes to use that knowledge to start his own photography business and make money doing what he loves. If his business never gets off the ground, he's settled knowing that his passion will always be there for photography.

Dragonfly

Photographer: Vinny Parreco

The Fall of a Flower

by Kendall M. Pearl

Lily Faust dug her booted feet into the ragged dirt road as her friends dragged her by her hands through the small town of Daray. The little town contained a total of thirteen double-story homes, each more dilapidated and rotten than the one before. Moss climbed the sides of the wooden walls like mountain climbers, clinging to every nook and cranny within the emerald green adventurer's reach and made it impossible to discern the color of the buildings. Many of the windows were broken and what remained was coated in a foggy film, softening the jagged edges of shattered glass. The town would have seemed completely devoid of life but for the browned, dead leaves tumbling across the road and the dancing shadows that grew as the sunlight died away.

"Come on, Lily," a feminine voice exclaimed.

Lily tore her gaze from the shadows and turned her attention back to fighting the grips of her friends. Her unkempt hair obscuring her vision slightly but allowing her to see the figure by her side. Holding onto her right arm was Amaia – a spritely, little, blue-eyed blonde that stood about five feet tall. Her platinum blonde curls bobbed around her small head teasing her shoulder blades. Amaia absolutely despised the thought of long hair, but also detested the notion of chopping all the beautiful curls off. Despite her small and fragile appearance, Amaia had quite the attitude to go with her pixie-like face. So much so, that even her parents did whatever they could to avoid an unnecessary argument with her and her petulant tantrums were infamous back home. Yes, Amaia was the clichéd and opulent Queen Bee of the town. Her parents gave into her every whim, including a credit card and a brand new, electric blue Bugatti. However, this was one situation in which Lily was not fully opposed to attempting argument against Amaia's latest stroke of "genius."

Her left hand had been captured in the relentless grasp of a large tan hand belonging to her friend, Kieran. He was the star quarterback of their hometown team, the Herons. His unwavering fortitude on the field turned him, in the eyes of the town, into a hero the likes of Beowulf or Achilles. He was generally loved by everyone. He was extremely tall with a muscular build. Long dark waves of brown hair hung over his brilliant sapphire blue eyes. He never said much outside of the field and when asked why, he simply declared, with a small smile and a roll of his gentle eyes, that he would appreciate not being carped all day just because he has nothing to say. Right then, his half-hidden eyes were squinting ahead with determination as he performed most of the work in towing Lily onward without saying a word.

"I don't know if this is a good idea guys," Lily began, protesting plaintively, her short legs protesting the sudden workout of fighting the strength of Amaia and Kieran combined. "This place looks as if no one has lived here for centuries and this magical –" *Or rather horrendous*, she thought. "– tower you guys want to go to can't really be in the best of shape to be climbing. I think we should just leave and go back home. I'll even pay for all of the gas to get there as long as we go *now*." Hopelessly, Lily tugged once more on the death-grips her friends had caught her in. No luck. Amaia and Kieran simply acted as if she had never tried to oppose them and kept on walking.

"Look, Lily," Amaia began with a pert flip of her hair. "You need to get over this silly little phobia of yours. We will be there with you the entire time, nothing will happen, and you will see that heights aren't that big of a deal." With that, the two bullying friends dragged Amaia past the final dilapidated house and around the bend. There it was, the exemplification of Lily's nightmares, the scenic tower Amaia and Kieran were so excited to make her climb.

Lily gaped at the towering mass of ancient stone and near fossilized wood. Just thinking about climbing to the top of that endless tower had Lily trembling with an inescapable feeling of fear as she pictured herself falling from the observation deck at the top, one false step sending her to her doom. Her heart began to thud rapidly in her chest, her lungs constricted into two tiny, deflated balloons, and her vision began to swim in and out of complete darkness. Amaia finally managed to avert her gaze and instead focused on the base of the tower.

There, hundreds of flower clusters danced gracefully like ballerinas in an unseen breeze sent by the early Autumn. Lily gazed in awe at the multitudes of lilac-stained rhododendrons; the pale, white faces of anemones as they turned their black noses to the air; and the beautiful emerald leaves of basil. Though beautiful, there was something eerie about the small, wild garden as Kieran and Amaia trampled several of the poor plants to reach the tower's door, invisible to the three as it was covered by over a decade's worth of vines and dust. Kieran temporarily released Lily's arm and grabbed two handfuls of the vines, tearing them down with a force that could match that of a Grizzly. The door was revealed to be crafted from strong oak, the wood appeared to have barely felt the effects of time since it was abandoned.

The aged door put up some resistance at being opened but was quickly overwhelmed by Kieran's giant physique when he threw himself against it with some football technique Lily still didn't know the name of. The door gave in to Kieran's strength and a giant CRASH resounded as the door broke off its top hinge and hung broken at an odd angle. Soon, Lily found herself inside the building with a friend at each arm once again.

The inside of the tower was dark, the only light emanating from the doorway. The air felt damp and smelled of mildew, like the crawlspace under a house after a large rainstorm., creating an atmosphere of unease that had hairs rising on the groups' necks. Lily could hear Kieran's light panting after his assault on the door as well as her own, slightly panicked breaths. Lily focused on Amaia's breathing as it kept a steady and soothing pace, allowing Lily to slowly calm herself and distract her from the prospect of climbing up to the top of the observation tower.

Kieran pulled three aluminum mini-flashlights from his pocket and dispersed them among the group. Soon, three beams of light were fluttering about in the dark, revealing a round, bare room devoid of decorations or furnishings of any kind. The wood plank walls were stained a dreadful shade of brown, poorly imitating mahogany, and the floors were designed in the same fashion. At the group's left began the rickety, metal staircase that led to the observation deck at the topmost level of the tower.

Lily barely had time to brace herself before her friends began to drag her forward once again. The planks of the floor groaned in protest as the weight of three teenagers burdened their retired forms. Lily grimaced with distaste and unease when the first step creaked and threatened to warp under the unwelcome weight and with each additional step, she felt herself become tenser and agitated as she envisaged the steps snapping beneath her feet, sending her plummeting back to the base of the tower with broken bones or worse.

They had finally reached the top after about ten minutes of the grueling, 3,000 step journey. Lily's erratic heartbeat was faster than the Greek god Hermes could fly on his winged sandals. Amaia and Kieran had ushered her to the edge of the platform and pointed out at the scenery below them. The trees and the small, abandoned town bathed in the soft, bluish light.

"Kieran, where did you put the bag?" Lily heard Amaia and Kieran move away from her and the edge of the balcony, but she paid them no heed, enamored by the sight before her. She sighed, wishing that she could stare out from that balcony forever.

Just as she heard a faint click and a slide of metal behind her, she remembered her fear of heights. Some unknown force seemed to compel Lily to drop her eyes and, suddenly, she was looking at the 3,000-step drop below her. Her stomach sank with dread and Lily felt the blood drain from her face, making her shiver with the sudden cold. Her heart skipped a few beats and her vision blackened around the edges as Lily was overcome with vertigo. She forced her clenched hands to release the rail and veered toward the door.

Her hands clutched frantically at the cool metal handle and she tugged. The door remained steadfast in its closed position, refusing to budge a single inch. Lily let out a strangled cry as she tugged harder on the unrelenting door and terror overtook rationality in her mind. She began banging on the oak and crying like a frightened child in high-pitched wails. "Amaia! Kieran! Let me out, let me out. Letmeoutletmeoutletmeout!" No one answered her cries for help and Lily feebly fell to the floor of the balcony, arms wrapped tightly around her knees, shivering in the growing chill as she cried softly to herself. Hope lay shriveled in her chest like a decaying corpse.

"You are giving up? Just like that?" a deep, sinuous voice inquired. Lily's head shot up and she looked desperately around her, but she saw no signs of anyone on the balcony.

"H-h-hello, is anyone there?" The shriveled form of hope stirred weakly in her chest as she waited for a response. A response she received.

"Yes, Lily. I am right here with you. Now, would you like my help escaping this dreadful tower?"

"Y-yes, please," Lily stammered. All she cared about was getting down.

"Alright, close your eyes. Imagine you are at the bottom of the tower, and it will be so." Lily did as the voice asked, visualizing her feet steady upon the earth once more.

When she opened her eyes, she rubbed her hands over her lids. She was on the ground again! Lily looked behind her to catch a glimpse of the door to the tower before she averted her gaze and looked around, hoping she would see some sign of Amaia or Kieran. All she felt was a desire to go home and pretend that nothing had ever happened.

"So, you're just going to let those to traitors get away with that? Act as if nothing ever happened?" The voice sounded as if it were now inside of Lily's head, but she dismissed the discovery as a side effect of an adrenaline rush. Then she started to think about what the voice had said. At those words, Lily's thoughts shifted to the top of the tower when she heard Amaia and Kieran leave. Before, Lily had assumed – no hoped – that it was all just some sort of mistake, that Amaia and Kieran had not meant to trap her on top of that tower. But now, the voice's words had forced her to see the truth. Amaia and Kieran had abandoned her to her fear intentionally. They had left her all alone when she had needed them most.

"They did leave you, didn't they? After all the time you spent together as the best of friends, you would think you could trust them more. I would bet right now those two are laughing at you! 'Ha ha ha! Did you hear Lily screaming? Let me out! Let me out!'" Lily jumped when she heard Amaia's voice so clearly. Then, she began to feel angry and betrayed. How could they do that to her? Kieran, who had defended her against bullies in the second grade and Amaia who had taught her to have fun every once in a while.

Amaia looked out where she knew Daray stood and reached to her side where she found her purse. She remembered where Amaia's precious Bugatti was parked. Turning one last time to the tower, Lily walked to the door and knelt. Reaching out a hand that would no longer shake she picked three stems from the wild garden, one rhododendron, a porcelain white anemone, and a small cluster of basil leaves, before tucking her hair behind her ear and securing it in place with the small bouquet. Then she stood and walked towards the people that had destroyed her trust, her hand now tucked delicately in her purse, stroking a small, folded object she had bought as a back-up to her untouched can of pepper spray.

She would teach them what it meant to make a fool out of her if it was the last thing she did.

....
.....

Epilogue
5 Years Later

Lily sat in the corner of the her own, pillow-soft room on her own little cot, humming some unknown tune with a faraway smile on her face. The whole room was probably about nine feet high and each wall was about twenty feet wide. Everything was white as freshly fallen snow: the windows, walls, floors, the cot with its sheets and pillow, the locked door, and even the clothes Lily wore every day. The only color in the room resided in Lily's unfailingly pink-tinged skin and her once-innocent green eyes. Her hair had grown dull from the hours spent in the lit but sunless room, but that didn't faze her. She remained in a state of perfect happiness.

There was a soft clink and Lily looked over to the door as it opened to reveal a hunched figure, also in white. "How are we today, Miss Faust?" The doctor's balding and wrinkled head shined in the light of the room as the old man shuffled his way through the doorway. Letting the steel door close behind him with an echoing click. His pale blue eyes shifted around the room nervously, attempting to avoid eye contact with his patient, his frail hands shivering almost imperceptibly in fear, the cup of water in his right hand nearly spilling water on the floor. The only thing he could think of in her presence was the horrid photos included in her files. Two figures lying limp in the front seats of a Bugatti, the interior painted a glistening crimson. He could not forget the words of the arresting policeman as he escorted her into the hospital. *"She just sat there laughing, as if it were all just some joke that she had just stabbed her two best friends to death. As if it were nothing of consequence, a normal everyday thing."* Dr. Boeman swallowed, as a lump formed in his throat, his instincts telling him to run for his life.

Lily smiled and giggled at the man's antics. "I am doing just wonderfully today! And Asura is doing great as well, though he said if we don't get out to see the sun soon, he may start to go mad. How are you today Dr. Boeman?"

At the mention of the second name, the old man only grew more nervous and shifted from foot to foot. "I-I am doing well. Thank you for asking. I have your medicine here, young lady. Now, you are going to take it this time correct?"

"You know I always take my medicine," Lily replied with a roll of her eyes, reaching out one hand for the little pills the doctor brought out from his pocket and the other for the cup of water. With a flamboyant flair, Lily popped the pills into her mouth and gulped down a mouthful of water. She then opened her mouth and lifted her tongue to show the doctor her empty maw. "See? All gone."

As soon as Dr. Boeman had confirmed that she had swallowed the medicine, he walked swiftly across the room and knocked twice. The door opened a crack and the old man slipped through the door and disappeared, the steel trap closing Lily into the room once more. However, she was not alone, so this did not bother her in the slightest.

Lily felt no prying eyes, so she turned her head and spat two tiny white objects behind her cot, into the farthest corner of the room. She leaned over the edge to see the somewhat large pile of various medications the doctors had tried to make her take over the past five years. Lily stared at them for a moment then sighed. "Asura, you know we will have to find another way to get rid of these soon. I can't keep hiding them behind my bed forever, you know."

"Don't worry. We won't be here too much longer," her best companion replied, still invisible to Lily as the day they had met five years prior. "There is going to be a new patient transferred here soon. They are to be placed into this room, which means that they will have to move you. When that time comes, we will make our escape."

"If you were able to leave and hear all those things, why didn't you just go outside? I know how you want to see the sun again," Lily pouted.

"What is the point of seeing the sun after all of this time if I cannot share my rediscovery with the one who freed me from that tower in the first place? We will escape together and see the sun again." The voice turned yearning as if the way out were just out of reach.

"Do you promise?" Lily closed her eyes and imagined the warmth of the lights in her room were the welcoming rays of the sun. She could feel the grainy dirt and the soft blades of grass under her bare feet as the wind tugged at her unruly brown hair that had been cut just above her shoulders. She could see the bright blue sky as brilliant as a sapphire, white clouds dotting the skyline as they imitated elephants and butterflies and any other object one could think of. She could smell the aroma of sweet flowers wafting through the air and hear birds chirping their tunes in a glorious harmony.

"Of course, I promise Lily. Have I ever lied to you?"

"No, you never have. Asura, could you sing me a song?" She heard a pause as Asura contemplated a tune and then she heard Asura's soft humming flow though the bare room.

Willow trees, a dancing breeze
Moonlight through the night
Watch your step or you shall find
A trap made by my kind
A shade of dark, a shade of night
Terror to bring you fright
If you delay, you shan't escape
The burning of the night.

Kendall M. Pearl is a current Chesapeake College student who is attending college for her Bachelor's Degree in English. She wants to become an editor or publisher. Kendall says her third grade teacher is the reason she loves to read and write so much. She saw how much Kendall hated the dull, monotonous stories the school provided through the common core curriculum and challenged her with novels that had her enthralled with the first page. Since then, Kendall never goes anywhere without at least one book to accompany her on her daily travels.

Thomas Point Lighthouse
Located in Maryland's Chesapeake Bay

Photographer: Rachael Kamm

Rachael Kamm is a current student at Chesapeake College. She is 18 years old and a self-taught photographer. Rachael is from the Eastern Shore of Maryland and loves to capture the beauty of the world around her. She started taking pictures at the age of 11 and really became interested in photography by the age of 14. When she was 16, Rachael got her first DSLR camera and she never leaves home without it.

Blue Bird
by Laura A. Lord

I'm a little blue bird
stowed in a jar,
and someone has left me
to tick away at the holes in the lid –
stuck in the limbo between
top shelf and dust filled corners.
I think they were expecting a transition –
pig pink worm to butterfly,
but I'm the loose ligament
of a buzzard's broken wing
and I'm skip hopping my ugly
back and forth in the mirrored glass.
I need a little less accountability here
and a little more darkness.
Close my eyes.
I'm a little blue bird
and I don't need the daylight
that brightens the sharp edges of my reflection.
I need my little glass jar,
the holes in my lid,
my ugly little dance,
and the darkness.

Laura A. Lord is an author and poet from the Eastern Shore of Maryland. She is a graduate of Chesapeake College and the current Editor in Chief of The Beacon. Laura is married and has three children.

Slowly Drifting

Photographer: Josh Anderson

Maryland's State Flower:
The Black-Eyed Susan

Photographer: Rachael Kamm

Waiting
By Dianna Greene

No matter how hard I try,
you'll never see my efforts.
The constant, late night messaging about stupid questions,
the persistent run ins in the hallway that I'd tell you was
coincidental
or even when I make sure to find a seat next to yours.

You'll never understand what I go through just to get you to notice
me.
You'll never care about me like you care about her –
That girl, who is the reason why you're up all night waiting for a
message.
That girl, who is the reason why you walk alone in the halls.
That girl, who is the reason why there's an empty seat next to
yours.

Not once did it cross your mind that maybe, just maybe, I was the
one for you,
but that's okay. One day you'll realize that I've been here for you all
along,
and when that day finally comes around, I'll still be here waiting
for you.

Dianna Greene is a senior at Colonel Richardson High School. She has been a dual enrollment student with Chesapeake College for the past two years. Dianna is a member of Colonel's National Honor Society, Spanish Honor Society, Spirit Club, Student Government Association, and wind ensemble, just to name a few. Once she graduates, she plans to major in Biochemistry at St. Mary's College of Maryland and transfer to Massachusetts College of Pharmacy and Health Sciences to earn her PharmD. Dianna lives in Federalsburg, Maryland with her mother.

The Cage
by Alanah Filion

She sits there in silence
on the cold, hard, empty floor of the cage –
long where she has lain many times before.
Marks all around her wrist and ankles from where the chains lie,
only to hear faint thumping on the inside.
"To bet set free," she whispers.
She sits up, ever so curiously, wondering what's beyond the chains.
She can see the door of the cage is open, but nothing else except
darkness.
The thumping grows louder and faster as her curiosity grows.
"To be set free!" She cries out.
She struggles time after time to get away from the thumping,
but never succeeding.
It just continues to grow louder and louder,
the thumping constantly growing.
Her constant struggles finally setting her free –
she hears the snap of the chains.
The only thing she can do is run,
never looking back.
Her footsteps and the thumping go together:
thump thump, thump thump, thump thump...
She runs until her feet can't touch the ground.
She leaps.
"To be set free," she whispers, one last time,
as she falls into an abyss of darkness.

Alanah Filion is a current student at Chesapeake College. She writes, "I was thrown into the dark at a young age, but I have persevered through it. Writing has been my passion and helped me through the tough times.

Finding My Passion
by Marissa Moldoch

Ever since I was a kid, I liked to write stories. My stories usually centered around a girl who went on an incredible adventure or found her true love. Though most of my stories went unfinished, I enjoyed the process of dreaming up a character and making their story come to life. As much as the thought of being a storyteller fascinated me, I never liked English class in elementary school. I always struggled with reading comprehension quizzes, and the grammar rules seemed to get tougher to remember every day. Did I really need to know how to find the direct object in the sentence? Then, in seventh grade, something clicked. I had an amazing English teacher, Mrs. Jones, who not only taught me the grammar rules, but taught me how to apply them to my writing. Soon, I learned how to think critically while I was reading and how to properly structure an essay. I continued to sharpen my skills as I progressed through high school, and English became more exciting as I used all the new techniques I had been taught.

After graduating from high school and arriving at Chesapeake College, I still wasn't sure what I wanted to major in. I knew I loved to read and write, but I wasn't sure if pursuing an English degree was the right option for me. What could I do with an English degree besides teach an English class? Many times, when I expressed an interest in pursuing an English degree to the people in my life, I received disappointing responses; they gently reminded me that becoming an author or a journalist was not going to be an easy task, and they constantly said that a job in either of those fields would prove to be unstable. I felt disheartened, and I repressed my enthusiasm for writing. I started to tell people that I might study Business in college since it seemed like that was what they wanted to hear. I even tried to convince myself that I should declare a Business major, since it sounded so impressive. However, I couldn't persuade myself to make such an extreme jump from English to Business, so I declared a Liberal Arts and Sciences major.

I enrolled in English 101, and I quickly realized the class was going to be right up my alley. The teacher encouraged me to hone my writing skills further, and she allowed me to express my creativity when I was given an assignment to write a story about my life. Most people were excited to leave English 101 behind, but I was disappointed; I truly enjoyed the class, and I couldn't wait to sign up for English 102. This should've been the biggest hint that I was meant to pursue English, but I still wasn't convinced that it was my calling. I put the thought of possibly pursuing an English degree in the back of my mind, and I continued to tell people that I would probably study Business when I transferred to a four-year college.

I enrolled in English 102 the following semester, and it quickly became my favorite class. I was introduced to new pieces of short fiction, drama, and poetry. I couldn't believe all the thought that went into writing a good story; authors took the time to incorporate irony, figures of speech, and rhyming schemes into their works to enhance the text. English 102 gave me a new appreciation for literature, and I became more convinced that English was the right path for me. I was worried, however, that I wouldn't be able to find a good job with an English degree. All the doubts that had been planted in my mind about studying English were starting to resurface, and I wasn't sure what to think. At the end of the semester, my teacher asked me if I was going to take any more English classes, and I expressed my interest in the subject. She encouraged me to follow my passion, telling me that I had a talent for writing. She opened my eyes to all the jobs available to English majors, the most interesting to me being the job of an editor. After hearing her kind words, I was inspired to make the choice to pursue an English degree.

I plan to transfer to Salisbury University to finish my education, and I am hopeful that I will be able to find an exciting job that allows me to read, write, and edit. Since declaring my desire to attain my English degree, I have received nothing but support from my friends and family. In fact, I have had two people offer to arrange meetings for me with local writers and editors they know. Looking back, I'm not sure why it took me so long to realize my passion for English. I'm glad I didn't let the concerns of others dissuade me from pursuing the subject that thrills me the most. I couldn't imagine my life without the fun of reading a captivating book or the therapeutic feeling of writing an interesting story.

Marissa Moldoch is a graduate of Chesapeake Christian School and a freshman at Chesapeake College. She hopes to transfer to Salisbury University next year to pursue and English degree. Marissa enjoys watching Orioles baseball, whether they're hitting home runs or striking out. She loves taking trips to Walt Disney World and has been to "The Most Magical Place on Earth" several times. Marissa can't wait to visit again soon.

Noise Machine
by Laura A. Lord

I have never been good at performing background music for
anyone.
I have too strong of a desire to hit the high notes.
I want to captivate,
somehow,
in stunning silence.
I want to please
without ever having to open my lips.
I want your awestruck envy
pooling as heavy smoke
running parallel my little pink tongue.
I want your nerves lit,
fireworks spilling their guts in the night.
I want, I want, I want...
I want to be more than a white noise machine on your bedside
table,
thumping out the heartbeat of some mystic jungle –
I want, I want, I want...

Shocked

Photographer: Melissa Comfort

"The Coma"

by E. C. Collins

D: "Good news, Mrs. Sanger. Thanks to a recent advance in cognitive activity scans, we can now predict when your son will wake up from his coma. We're predicting roughly nine months."

S: "Nine months? That's a long time."

D: "Oh it's not so bad, Mrs. Sanger. You will find having your child mature into an upstanding gentleman quite worth it, I believe. Why, my Jeremy recently turned 23 and is currently planning his marriage ceremony. A lovely girl, don't you know. Her name is J—"

S: "Yes, yes, I'm sure it's lovely. It's just... well, the medical bill will be exorbitant, won't it?"

D: "Mrs. Sanger, this is a life we're talking about. Please consider what you say before you say it. But if that's really such a concern for you, there's no need to fear. There are programs in place to help you."

S: "Programs?"

D: "Oh, certainly. I assure you, you won't go hungry because of this. The government will be sure of that."

S: "But it will be rather inconvenient, won't it?"

D: "Inconvenient? Well, I suppose it will be a little—"

S: "If it's all the same to you, then, why don't we just cut off life support? I really can't be bothered right now. I'm attending college, you know, and I have a bright future ahead of me."

D: "This is nothing to joke about, Mrs. Sanger."

S: "Good thing I'm not joking, doctor."

D: "Surely you won't kill your child because of finances!"

S: "It's more than that, doctor. After he awakes I shall have to help him learn to walk—you said yourself there will be considerable atrophy—I shall even have to help him eat! It's just too much. Much better to pull the plug."

D: "Do you find this amusing? I don't like morbid humor. I've seen too much death to find it funny."

S: "I'm not joking."

D: "Well, you certainly aren't being serious."

S: "I am."

D: "Then you're insane!"

S: "I am quite sane, doctor, and I have resolved to take him off life support. If you cannot reconcile the two, I fear the problem is with you."

D: "We're getting nowhere. Quit this morbid talk so we can move along."

S: "I will not."

D: "Well, it hardly matters. You can't do it."

S: "Why not?"

D: "It's murder, that's why!"

S: "Murder? Haven't you heard? Legislation has been passed. Anyone who does not meet the standards of personhood is subject to termination if their guardian deems it appropriate. He does not meet their standards."

D: "Absurd. I've heard no such thing."

S: "He lacks cognitive capacity."

D: "Lacks cognitive capa— Perhaps he does now, but he won't in nine months!"

S: "Look, this is all very tiring, doctor, and I have an exam tomorrow. I assure you, the law is on my side. I will submit my decision to your superior if you refuse to accept it."

D: "I'm giving you one more chance to admit the ruse, so we can both have a good laugh."

S: "There is no ruse, doctor."

D: "But it's murder!"

S: "I have the right to choose."

D: "Do I have the right to choose to kill you? I have a scalpel in my drawer. I could draw it out."

S: "Are you threatening me?"

D: "No, I'm trying to reason with you!"

S: "In that case, no. I have cognitive capacity."

D: "In nine months so will he!"

S: "We've already been here."

D: "Nine months, Mrs. Sanger! Is potential for personhood worth nothing?"

S: "I'm done talking to you. You're hopeless."

D: "Hopeless? Because I won't agree with you implicitly I'm hopeless?"

S: "No, because you won't listen to reason."

D: "You haven't presented reason!"

S: "I can choose whether I want to accept this burden or not. It's a basic human right. You obviously can't understand that. That's why you're hopeless."

D: "I can't believe—"

S: "I don't care what you can believe. I have nothing left to say to you, doctor. Good day."

Fin

Somewhat obsessed with the English language, Cody has been an avid reader since his youth. An aspiring copyeditor, Cody is currently attending Chesapeake Community College for his Associate's in Liberal Arts and Sciences. His hobbies include reading, writing, learning more about the world, and taking long walks in God's wonderful creation.

Sin-Eater
by Laura A. Lord

I knew when they found my Da, face-down in the grass with the sun frying the top of his shining head like a tomato that they were going to call in the Sin-Eater. The sound of the lawnmower idling brought the shrill sound of my mother's screaming down to a bearable level. I suppose she was crying, though it didn't sound like it. It sounded angry and looked like praying with her there on her knees in the dirt. My brother was crying – big, soft, round tears that ran quietly down his cheek and got stuck in the bright copper tangles of hair on his chin. My sister was leaning against him. I couldn't tell if she was crying. Her face was dug deep into his shoulder and her body was jerking as if she had the hiccups.

I thought I should cry. I thought there must be something wrong with me, but I just stood there and stared and wondered to myself if there was dirt in his teeth. My tongue grew dry at the thought and I ran it across the stubbly plaque on my teeth, imagining it was sand and grit and not just a night's worth of sleeping with my mouth hanging open like a dog out a window. I wondered if they were going to lift him up out of the dirt or if we were just supposed to stand there and watch him.

The shadow from the tree was creeping over and by the time my grandmother poked her way across the yard the edge of that shadow was touching the sunburned skin of my Da's ear. I watched her thin arms grasping the edges of her walker and the tennis balls on its legs sink into the soft edges of my mother's garden.

"Didya call 'im?" she said, barely casting a glance to the prone display of her son-in-law below her.

My mother must have lost all of her words, because she just shook her head and sat there on the ground plucking out long stems of grass by the root.

"Get her inside, Sissy," Jonathan, my brother, said. "I'll get him."

I watched Sissy step over and reach under our mother's arms like she was helping our neighbor's little toddler up off his bottom. She lifted our mother up and turned to step into her side and hold her tight. They walked this way, haphazardly across the yard, with my grandmother following a few paces behind.

Jonathan went to the shed behind mother's garden and grabbed the big blue tarp we used to cover the mower in the winter and he drug it over and covered my Da with it. Now there was a big blue lump in our yard and we stood there and stared at it and I still thought I ought to cry about the whole thing. It just didn't seem like it was going to happen.

"Can I go to Nancy's and play?" I asked.

Jonathan startled and looked down, as if he just noticed I'd been standing there the whole time.

"Shit, Maddie." He bent and took the faded Yankees cap off his head. He smacked it against his knee and ran dirty fingers through his matted hair. "I'm sorry, girl. You okay?"

I just stared at him. I didn't want to say I was fine. You weren't supposed to be fine when this sort of thing happened. I scrunched my eyes tight and put my hands behind my back. I pinched my arm hard and kept thinking the saddest things, but it was like my eyes just wouldn't work with me. I couldn't cry about it and I thought Jonathan was going to be mad when I opened them all clear. Instead, Jonathan hugged me tight and I could smell the thick scent of oil and exhaust on his neck from the shop where he worked.

"Go on to Nancy's for a bit and tell her Da to come on over. I'm gonna need help getting him ready for the Sin-Eater."

"You gotta call him?" I asked.

Jonathan nodded his head and then pulled his cap on tight and down, so it buried his eyes in shadow. He stood up and walked back to the shed, closing the door behind him. I looked back at the house and saw through the kitchen window my grandmother at the stove and a column of steam rising from the cracked kettle. My mother and Sissy were at the table, their heads pressed together, and I thought again that they might be praying. I wanted to go get my doll to take to Nancy's, but I didn't feel much like praying.

*****

Nancy's Da was outside loading chopped blocks of wood into the back of an old orangey-red pick-up truck. I grabbed the side and used the hub cap to push myself up onto the side of the truck. Nancy was on the other side and every time her Da threw a log in she would grab it and stack it nice and neat in the back. He tossed one in and waved hello to me as I grabbed it before Nancy could and slid it onto the stack.

"Ain't you headed to church in a bit, Maddie girl?" he asked.

"Nah, sir. We can't be going to church this morning as Jonathan's out calling the Sin-Eater." A log banged against the back of the truck, bounced and fell against the side of the tire with a clunk.

"What you say?" He had climbed up the back of the truck bed and was almost in my face.

"Jonathan said he gonna need your help, 'cause of them having to call the Sin-Eater."

"Who they callin' him for, girl?"

"Da." I said, looking over to see Nancy's thin little lips drop open. My grandma would have told her she was catching flies and snapped her fingers under her chin. I didn't want to look at her Da when I said it, though. I thought he'd want me to cry, too.

"Oh God!" He jumped off the back of the truck and headed inside, yelling behind him, "Nancy you stay with Maddie, now. You hear?"

"Yes, sir," she said.

We sat quiet in the truck for a minute while we listened to her Da talking to her Ma about heading over to my house. Nancy just sort of stared at me and toed a loose log back into place. It slid out and she pushed it in again and again, making this annoying scraping sound on the bed of the truck.

"Wanna go get your dolls?" I asked. "I didn't get no chance to get mine."

"What'd he look like?" Nancy asked.

"Who?"

"The Sin-Eater."

"I ain't seen him yet. They're just now callin' him." I said.

"Oh," Nancy mumbled and jumped off the side of the truck. "So, what'd your Da look like?"

"Like dead," I said, jumping off my side and walking around to meet her at the front of the truck. We leaned on the hood and stared down the dirt of her lane. I kicked a small, white stone over to her and she pushed it back. In the backyard we heard a four-wheeler start up and knew her Da was driving over to my house. He'd pop out of the woods right by the tree with my tire swing hanging off it and from there he'd see that big, blue lump pressing into the ground.

"It looked like he was fat." I said.

"He was fat."

"Yeah, but like…like there was more of him. Like it was sinking down in the dirt." The breeze kicked up and pushed a long strand of dark hair into my face and against my lips. I pushed hair out with my tongue and shoved it back behind my ears.

"He was fat, though." Nancy said.

"Yeah, I know." I pushed off the truck and walked up to front porch. "I don't wanna talk about it, no more. I'm gonna go get the dolls."

"'Kay," she said, following me up the steps. The screen door slapped shut behind us and by the time we had dug to the bottom of her Ma's hope chest and gathered the dolls and the clothes around us, I'd forgotten all about my Da and the big, blue tarp and how fat he was, and the Sin-Eater.

*****

"Time for washin'," Nancy's Ma said, poking her head around the door. "Get that stuff picked up and let's get goin'."

I started scooping up dolls and putting them back in the chest. "I guess I'll go on home."

"No. Stay on here and get washed up," she said.

"I ain't got no clothes here."

Nancy's Ma went to the closet in the hall and pulled out two black dresses. "This 'un was Nancy's last year. She done past you now, so it ought to fit you right enough." She dropped the dresses on the bed and headed down the hall. After a moment we heard water splashing against porcelain and knew she was filling up the tub. Nancy tugged her doll's hair back into a ponytail while we waited, and I traced the pattern of lilies on the wood of the chest.

"You ain't past me that much," I muttered.

"Psshaw!" She laughed. "I got you by an inch or more. You just slow at growin'."

"I ain't slow."

"You always slow," she sneered. "And skinny."

Nancy could be like that – a bit meaner than she needed to be. She liked to be the best at everything, but she knew she was moving to the city soon, so she said she had to start acting like she wasn't country. I remember when I told my mother that and she laughed and said Nancy had country shoved so far up under her nails there weren't enough bleach in the whole of Grayson's Market to get it all out.

"Girls!" Nancy's Ma called. We both hopped up and ran, barefoot down the hall to the bathroom. The water was steaming and the small mirror over the sink had fogged up. We stripped out of our t-shirts and

44

shorts and plopped down in the water like sisters. Nancy helped scrub my hair, because it was so long and hard to reach. She didn't need my help with hers anymore, since she got the cooties last year and her Ma had to cut it all short. It was taking its time growing back and looked like a blonde lion's mane, all puffed out around her face.

Her Ma came in and checked us. She had rough fingers and pulled our ears out to the side and jabbed her fingernails under ours to scrape out the dirt. When we were out, wrapped in faded pink towels, she sat us on our knees between her legs and scraped a metal comb through our hair. I kept thinking I would look down and see a pile of brown hair at her feet every time she yanked through another knot. Finally, there we were: hair slicked back and straight and skin shining white.

"Go on and get dressed 'fore you catch a chill," she said.

It was easily ninety degrees out, and even after the bath, sweat was gathering under our arms and at the backs of our knees. No one was going to catch a chill today. I stared at the dress on the bed, with its long sleeves and high collar and gritted my teeth. Nancy was sliding into hers. It had a nice high waist and short sleeves. The collar was white and had a little button at the back that I fastened for her. It fell right above her knees and she looked so grown up for a minute that I forgot she was my age. The right dress could do that to a twelve-year-old girl. I tried on Sissy's prom gown, and even though it was dragging green silk on the ground, I looked like I was at least fourteen in it.

I struggled to pull the tight collar of my dress over my head and popped out of it like a turtle. Static shot through my hair and made the dry ends pop up. The sleeves were almost an inch too short and the dress was well above my knee.

"Guess you did grow a bit," Nancy admitted.

I stuck my tongue out at her and pulled at the edges of the sleeves. When they wouldn't come down any further, I shoved them up above my elbows.

"Turn around," Nancy said.

I did and pulled my hair off to the side while she worked the tie at the back. I pulled a quick braid through my hair to control the frizz and let it hang, loose-ended, off my shoulder. Nancy's Ma came in and shook her head at us.

"That's almost indecent," she said, eyeballing me. "It'll have to do. Come here and let me do that hair of yours."

She pushed me back to my knees in front of her and began pulling my hair into strict braids. One fell by my cheek and then she went to the other side and worked it. Her fingers moved fast, and she wasn't even watching her work. Instead she stared at Nancy and clucked her tongue.

"There ain't a thing I can do with that mop of yours. Teach you to be out playin' with the Hall boys. You wonderin' where you pick up cooties from...Well, there you go. Guess you won't be doin' that again."

She went on and on for a bit about the Hall boys and how bad they were, how they put firecrackers in the ladies' stall at the Waffle House in town and how they put turtles in the road for people to run over. I stifled a laugh. I knew Nancy liked to leave for school early, so she could meet me at the end of the lane. We'd head down the hill to school and right around the bend from my house the Hall boys would come jumping out of the woods like ghosts. They didn't scare us no more, but it was still fun, and no one knew we went walking with them to the school. They were in high school though, so we had to leave them there while we went to the middle school.

When my hair was pulled tight into two heavy braids, Nancy's Ma left the room. She was still mumbling about boys and cooties and Nancy was red-faced about the whole thing.

"Aw, don't let it get you," I said. "Those boys never gave me no cooties."

"You probably got 'em and don't even know it," Nancy spat out. "You don't even cut your hair never. Who knows what's up in there?"

I shut up quick and let her go. She was just mad about having to have her hair cut off. I scratched at my head. I didn't have no cooties. Nancy's Ma called us from the other room and said it was time to go. We both grabbed a doll from the chest and headed out to the kitchen.

*****

I didn't realize it was so late. Nancy's Da had cleaned out the truck of all the wood and Nancy and I climbed in the back and sat on a blanket in the bed. We could see the back of her parent's heads in the little window and knew they were talking, but the old rattle of the engine drowned it all out. It was too loud to talk to one another, so we just sat quiet and brushed our fingers through our doll's hair.

There were a lot of cars in my lane. Some of them were pushed off to the side. I saw a couple of four-wheelers out back. They looked awfully close to my mother's garden and I thought she would lose her mind when she saw that, but she was standing out on the porch, just staring at the backyard, not even caring that someone parked by her pole beans.

Jonathan was standing by her and there were people going in and out all over. The screen door kept slamming and I saw candles in the windows. Jonathan waved me over and I waved bye to Nancy before I climbed up the porch steps.

"Go hug Ma," Jonathan said, giving me a gentle pat on the back in her direction.

Ma had her hands wrapped around the porch railing. Her fingers looked like white claws. I'd never seen her so quiet. She wasn't just not speaking; she wasn't making any noise at all. I tapped her elbow lightly and when she didn't even move or look at me, I looked back at Jonathan. He waved his hands at me to go ahead and I quickly turned and hugged her hip, let go, and spun away from her.

"Alright, Maddie," Jonathan said. "Go on and find Sissy. I got to stay up here and wait for him to get here."

"Who else is gettin' here?" I asked. It looked like the whole town was in my house. I even saw the man who cut Da's hair every Saturday morning and the brown lady who delivered mail in the afternoons in those tiny blue shorts all the postmen wore.

"The Sin-Eater is comin'."

I thought I ought to go find Nancy and let her know that he'd be coming in at the back porch where Jonathan was, but he told me to find Sissy. I opened the screen door to the kitchen and walked in. Grandma was sitting at the end of the table in my Da's spot. She had a full ashtray in front of her and a nub of a cigarette shoved between her lips. The end was bright orange and smoke had billowed up around her like part of her hairdo.

"Where you been, girl?"

"I was at Nancy's, Grandma," I said.

"Ain't right. You ain't a kid no more; you should've been here. Get in there and say bye to your Da."

"I got to find, Sissy," I started.

"You got to do what you're told," Grandma interrupted.

I nodded and followed her stiffly pointed finger into the next room. The blue tarp was gone and instead someone had put out the tablecloth with the big red poinsettias on it. My Da laid out on it like he was the Christmas turkey, dressed up in his church pants and a white shirt. There was a thick slice of bread lying next to him on one of mother's wedding plates. A small pile of salt was gathered like a mountain rising out of the paisley print on the edge and a matching glass was full of wine as dark as Welch's grape juice.

I looked over and saw Nancy and her Ma and Da standing on the other side of the table. Nancy cried ugly. Her face was all scrunched up and red, snot was running out of her nose and I thought she really looked country now. I squeezed my eyes shut again and tried to force out some tears. I didn't want anyone to see me not crying. Maybe they'd think I was saying bye this way. Honestly, I didn't know how to say bye to someone who wasn't going to say it back. When trying to make tears didn't work, I turned and ran through the back of the house, avoiding my grandmother in the kitchen. My boots clomped heavy on the ground and I tripped around all the people crowded in our little living room, before escaping out the front door and into the night air.

It was quiet out front. Everyone was in the house or out back waiting on the Sin-Eater to come. I sat on the front steps and thought back to Sunday school and my teacher, Ms. Little. She was an odd woman, with bony arms and big hair. She wore it curled up on top of her head like a turban and tucked her big, pink glasses into it when she was inside. My mother said her skirts were too tight, but she always wore a thick black belt at the top of them that seemed to be helping to hold her up. She was real top-heavy and every button-down shirt she wore seemed to be right on the edge of splitting wide open.

Ms. Little had taught our Sunday School class for three or four years, since the old teacher died. She liked to talk about the Sin-Eater. She'd had to call one in for her husband when he died and ever since then she was obsessed with talking about him. Ms. Little told us how important they were, that if we ever were to die all alone somewhere and no priest got to us in time, we'd need that Sin-Eater there to make sure we were all clean for heaven.

It never made much sense to me, how someone was going to eat some bread and suddenly the dead person would be all forgiven and ready for heaven. I wondered what my Da had to be forgiven for? He liked his routine and every night before bed he would kneel in his boxer shorts and white tank top. He'd bow his head down on his hands and pray soft and low as an engine in the distance. What sin could he have done between waking up and going out to mow the lawn?

I was still sitting there on the porch when I heard the rustling sounds over by the window. I thought there might be a possum back there or raccoon and climbed carefully off the steps. I pushed up against the house and peeked around the corner at the horde of forsythias my mother had planted along the side. I noticed Sissy's leg first. It was so bright and white and bare out in the moonlight, it practically shone like the long beam of a flashlight. Her skirt was pushed up high around her hips and I looked up to see a strong hand pressed tight against her mouth. She wasn't looking at me, but instead at whatever face she saw inside the dark hood of the man who held her. He was moving between her legs, dancing against her.

I couldn't tell if Sissy were crying or just trying to talk behind his hand, but he wasn't letting go. A rhythmic grunting sound came from behind the hood and after a few moments he seemed to collapse against her. His body pressed her completely against the wall and I thought she was going to get those white marks from the siding all over her shirt. Suddenly, he stepped back and Sissy collapsed to the ground like someone had cut her strings. She fell in a tangle of elbows and knees and I could tell then she was crying. Her body was heaving hiccups again.

"I will absolve your sin, girl," a voice said, crawling dark and filth. I shuddered and the hair on my arms stood up with gooseflesh. I ducked down to the ground, positive he was going to see me. I watched as he bent and brushed the hair from Sissy's face. She startled and shied away from him, but he gripped her chin in his tight fingers and pushed his hood back. His face was long and his teeth were broken and black. His jaw looked as if it had been broken and set again poorly, like the teeth wouldn't quite meet up if he tried to bite them together. He held her face tight and bent down to kiss her. I watched his tongue slide into her mouth and then heard her yelp. When he released her, blood dripped heavy from her bottom lip.

By the time I looked back to him, he was gone. Sissy was burying herself into the dirt behind the bushes. She had scrambled up against the wall and was hiding her face in her arms. I sat and watched her while she cried. Eventually her tears subsided to the steady beat of hiccups and sniffling. She tugged at her skirt and brushed at the white marks on her shirt. When she stood, I quickly backed up and rushed around the corner to the porch. I didn't want her to know I had seen her sin.

When she came around the corner her eyes grew big like a deer's. "How long you been there, Maddie?" She asked.

"I just come out," I stuttered.

She hid her face in her hands and quickly walked inside. I heard her on the steps and knew she had dodged the living room and gone straight upstairs to her room. I stood there, catching my breath, when the rest of the house seemed to come alive with activity. I hurried to the small window just as the man in the black cloak stepped in through the kitchen door. My brother was right behind him and together they made their way to the dining room. A single chair was brought out and placed down at my Da's side where the plate was set.

Jonathan handed the man a small, purple Crown Royal bag. I heard the rattle of change in it and wondered at the whole tradition of this spectacle. I wondered if he had to kiss my Da, too – to absolve his sins, or if he only had to do that to Sissy, because she had no bread. Before the man sat down at the table, everyone in the room turned their backs to him and bowed their heads. They stood silently as he pulled the hood from his face. His hair was thick and matted and his skin pot-marked with acne. He looked young, with big thick eyebrows that seemed to stretch all the way across his face. It made him look angry as he ripped the bread in half and shoved it into his mouth. He chewed slowly, while wiping the second half through the pile of salt. His mouth seemed to hurt him, certainly because of his teeth. I absentmindedly ran my tongue across the bright silver cap in my own mouth.

After a few moments he had finished with the bread and salt. He drank the wine quickly so that it ran down the corners of his long jaw and dripped on to the poinsettia table cloth. When he was done with the meal, he stood and laid a hand on my Da's chest. He bowed his head and said, "He is ready."

Just as quickly as he had come in, he was gone – out through the kitchen and headed through the back yard. I heard our priest's voice calling for prayer and I raced off the porch and around the side of the house. I saw him walking across the patch of grass where we'd found my Da. He was almost to the tire swing when I caught up with him.

"Wait!" I called under my breath.

He ignored me and continued forward, not missing a beat.

We were well into the woods when I tried calling to him again. "Sin-Eater! Wait!"

Again, he ignored me, but he picked up his pace. The cloak flew out behind him as he turned swiftly around the large trunk of an old poplar. I ran to catch up with him, swinging around the tree trunk and scraping my hand on the bark. I came around so fast I plowed right into his chest, knocking myself off my feet and onto the ground. I felt the sharp stick of a branch against my leg and the hot warmth of a cut that opened there.

"What?" He growled.

"Is that it?" I asked. "Is my Da gonna be in heaven now?"

"I said he is ready."

"And Sissy? 'Cause you didn't eat no bread with her..."

"You saw me tonight," he said.

"Everyone saw you. You were in my house."

He shook his head and bent down to balance on the balls of his feet. "No. You saw me with that woman."

I nodded. "My sister."

He pushed his hood back and stared at me with dark eyes.

"You watched us."

I nodded again.

"Did you go to her, after?" He asked.

I turned my head and looked back the way we had come. Suddenly he grabbed my chin, like he had Sissy's, and roughly yanked me back to face him.

"Did you go to her?" He repeated.

"No. I ran back to the porch." I admitted.

"What else did you watch?" He asked.

"Nothin'. I didn't see nothin' else."

"You watched me eat."

My cheeks must have given me away. I felt them heat up and stain bright red. I tried to duck my chin away from him, but he held me tight, his fingers digging into my skin.

He nodded. "You have sinned. Your sister needed you and you turned your back to her. You ignored her pain...You watched me take sin."

I shook my head violently in his grasp. "Let go. I want to go back. Let go!"

He dropped my face and stood, grabbing my wrist and pulling me with him as he did.

"You have sinned."

"I will go back. The priest is there. I'll tell him..."

"No. You have sinned. I will absolve you."

He pulled me behind him and started to walk away from the direction of my house.

"No!" I yelled. "Let go!" My voice echoed and bounced off the trees. It came back at me swiftly, slapping me across the face. My eyes welled with tears and I thought he was going to pull my wrist from its socket.

He turned and swept me up over his shoulder. He began to run through the woods and I felt the snap of branches on my back as I screamed over and over into the heavy wool of his cloak. I tried to kick, but my legs were held tight in his hands. My fingers clawed at his back.

"You have sinned and so, you are mine, and so I will absolve you...in time." he laughed as he ran. The woods grew thick and the moonlight was snubbed out and his laughter rumbled against my stomach. Suddenly, I wanted my Da very much.

And I cried.

Love in a Lens

Photographer: Vinny Parreco

Spiraling Out of Control

Photographer: Josh Anderson

Youth
by Jacky Smith

We fought until sunrise
Forgave until noon
Loved each other
Underneath the moon
No more false promises
Or little white lies
Hold me and talk of tomorrow
For dreamers never die

Margarite
by Rob Dey

I had heard the story: a dark theater in Easton, the ballerina in the prime of her professional life and youth cut down in a pirouette of blood and left to rot in an elevator. I always hated how the elevator took her fame... just like the killer took her life. Both lived on, but not her. But what's a happy ending anyway?

I was alone in the elevator when the electric failed. The elevator came to an abrupt stop. After a few minutes the no smoking rule went out the window.

"There's no smoking in here," she said with a giggle.

Margarite. Well. At least I'm not alone in this damn thing anymore.

"How are ya dear?"

"Well, ya know...," she replied.

Small talk aside, it was looking to be a long time stuck here. I was getting antsy. I didn't like the prospect of being stuck here all night without my constant companion: nicotine. Margarite, on the other hand, didn't seem concerned as she bummed her sixth smoke from me in the last thirty minutes.

She slumped down next to me on the floor and met my gaze. I just had to ask.

"I know about you, but...what happened that night?"

"The night I died?"

"Yeah...I'm sorry. I shouldn't have asked," I said awkwardly. I felt like a goon, but she seemed entertained nonetheless.

"What did you hear?" she giggled.

"Well...basically, the doors of the elevator opened and there you were. Dead with a knife wound in your chest."

She giggled again. "And so, everyone assumes it was murder? Silly Sillies!"

"You killed yourself!?" I exclaimed, more than asked. Was this a twist to the tale of legend no one knew? A suicide!

Semi-exasperated, she asked, "If I killed myself, wouldn't the knife still be there?"

"So...you...Were you murdered?"

"A little of both, sugar. You see, life on the road left no time for romance, especially for a girl in those days. If a traveling girl like me picked the reputation of strumpet, well... I wouldn't be performing ballet anymore. Not any respectable kind anyway."

She bummed another cigarette and stared into the smoke with a faraway look. She continued. "I knew this. I accepted this. But I'm, I was, only human. There was this fellow here back then – dashing, debonair, a writer. I'm not telling who, a girl has to have her secrets and I'm telling you a big one as it is."

"I understand." I choked the words out in almost whisper, afraid to make a sound lest this all end. A ghost, real and in the flesh (figuratively speaking) telling me the real story of her death!

"Well, I fell head over heels for him and I confessed my affection. He, though, was the skittish sort. Couldn't believe I'd settle down and give up my, to this point, one and true love: ballet. I was intent to prove him wrong! I told him, for an embrace I'd cut off my fingers. For a kiss, my arms.

"Now, you also must know, he was a wiseass and I just adored that about him. So, he says to me, well...what would you give to spend the night? I looked him dead in the eye and said my heart. He says, prove it. What's a girl to do? I kept a little dagger in my garter, for protection. I knew he was falling, so I proved it!"

"What? How?" I asked, a bit confused.

In a sarcastic tone, she replied, "Well, I think you're denser than the smoke in here! Did anyone say how big the wound in my chest was?"

"But you said it yourself... f you'd killed yourself, where was the knife?"

"Oh sugar...he took it. He had to. It had my heart on it."

57

Rob Dey is a soon to be graduate of Chesapeake College and a writing tutor in the Academic Support Center. He enjoys gaming, history, Led Zepplin, and H.P. Lovecraft. His goals are to transfer to a four-year school and pursue a B.A. in creating writing.

Beauty, Death, and Decay
by Alanah Filion

She stands there, in all her beauty – winds whispering secrets through her hair.
Everyone knew her soul was far too good for this twisted world.
She was a bright light in a dark tunnel.
She always forgave and gave everyone a chance, even if it was death itself.
People always used, abused, and bruised her.
Her soul slowly diminished, like the light of a candle slowly burning out.
People took the light, little by little, until there was nothing left except darkness, and a bitter cold wind swept over the world.

Sandy Point Lighthouse
Located North of the Chesapeake Bay Bridge

Photographer: Rachael Kamm

Please Not Me
by Jacky Smith

Two tendrils,
from the same unruly plant,
grown together.
Twisting round each other,
ever upwards,
only together,
strong enough to weather the winds.
Which will it be,
after the wither,
left in a heap of untidy curls that fit none,
but the other?

A Twisted Turn
by Debra Jones

One Thursday evening, while sitting at home bored, a good friend of mine called and asked if I wanted to go with her to a friend's party. I told her I needed to find a provider to watch my children first. Eventually I called her back, saying, "Hey, let's go. I found a sitter". She exclaimed, "Yay!" We stayed on the phone for about another twenty minutes, chatting about what we were going to wear, where the party was being held, and, most importantly, who was going to be there.

Once I got off the phone, I began to prepare my children for bed, so that there was nothing much for the sitter to do besides be an adult in the home. After my children were asleep, I began to get myself ready to go out for the evening. I swear it seemed like I went through everything in my closet. Two hours later, I was ready for the party. I settled on wearing some light blue jeans, a mint green top, and some cute mint green shoes that I purchased about a month before and was dying to wear.

My friend arrived to pick me up around 10:30 PM. I kindly went over everything with my sitter, including letting her know how to contact me if there was an emergency, and that their dad would be home around 2:00 AM. I explained when he arrived, she could leave. Then I left the house. I remember sending a text message to my children's father saying I had gone to a party with Shakia and I'd be home before the sun came up. That was my beloved saying.

When Shakia and I arrived at the party, the outside was packed. I mean there was no place to park, and the line was wrapped around the building. I will never forget, it took us a good twenty-five minutes to get inside of the building. I kept repeating, "There must be somebody famous inside." I had never waited so long to get inside of any place, not even a restaurant. I guess my patience was getting the best of me. When we finally got inside, we walked straight to the back bar, and stayed there for about twenty-five minutes before walking around. A moment later, we found some friends we knew and began dancing with them.

The party let out at exactly 2:00 AM. Neither one of us were ready to go home, so we decided to hang out with a few friends for a while. I placed a call to one of my homeboys asking him if he was outside. He told me, "Yes." I replied, "Are you alone or is there someone with you?" To my surprise he responded, "Blue." Blue is the guy my friend just so happened to have a crush on. At that moment I knew we were going to have some fun. Whenever we linked up with these guys we always had a good time.

Shortly after arriving to my friend's neighborhood, Blue received a call and had to leave. Shakia and I got into the car, but were still not ready to go home, so we both decided to get some food. We were debating on what to eat and where to go. I decided that we should go to Denny's. Denny's is like the afterhours restaurant in Baltimore; if the club was popping then Denny's was popping. We were bound to have a good laugh from a drunk soul. Before going to Denny's, I had to use the restroom and Shakia's house was closer than mine, so we stopped there. When we pulled up to her apartment complex, she parked along the curbside, instead of in the parking lot. She stayed in the car and handed me her door keys to get into her apartment.

I got out of the car and walked up to her apartment building. There are two doors, one to enter the building and the other to her apartment. When she gave me the key, she put the apartment door key in my hand, because the front door didn't lock, due to it being broken. I proceeded into the building and walked down the steps. Unfortunately, as soon as I reached the door, I dropped the keys while doing the potty dance. I immediately picked up the keys and began to place them in the door one by one.

Suddenly, that front door swung open. I looked up and there was this young man entering the building. He was wearing a dirty white T-shirt, some blue jeans, and black boots. I proceeded with trying to find the right key to enter the apartment. That's when I heard footsteps. I looked up again, and now the boy was in my personal space. I said to him, "What?" He then reached to the side of his waist and pulled out one of the biggest kitchen knives I had ever seen. I said to him, "Drop the knife. We can fight." He never said a word and stabbed me in the neck. I responded by saying, "Shit, he's not playing." I pushed past the young man and ran up the steps. At the same time, he ran behind me, still stabbing at me. I remember, while running, getting stabbed on my left side. I never gave up running toward my friend and screaming for help.

As soon as I reached the passenger's side of the car, I fell. This young man stood over top of me and continued to stab me several more times. Eventually, he stopped, and my friend then got out of the car and helped me get off the ground and into the car. I remember my body feeling like it was on fire. I was covered in blood, scared to death, and didn't know if I was going to make it or not. Through all the pain I could hear my friend calling the police while screaming for help. I remember getting into the ambulance and asking the female EMT helping me, "Am I going to make it?" Her reply was, "I'm going to do all that I can do, so that you are okay." I closed my eyes and prayed.

Despite it all, I woke up in the University of Maryland Shock Trauma Center with seventeen four-inch stab wounds, all to the upper body, chest, neck, stomach, face, arms, shoulder, and left side; and five slices to my hands, because I used them as a shield. My chin was stitched and stapled back together. My family members, lots of doctors and nurses, and the police were all standing over me, some crying, and doctors trying to talk to me when I finally regained consciousness. I was lost for words and couldn't do anything but thank God I was alive. My biggest concern was my children, and not wanting them to see me in that condition. I had never met the boy before; he had escaped from an area psychiatric ward. To this day, I still wonder if I was set up by my so-called friend who did very little to help me survive the attack that changed my life forever.

Debra Jones is a freshman at Chesapeake College. She is a mother of seven, a grandmother of five, and is studying Criminal Justice. Debra is engaged to Jasmine Reece. She plans to transfer to Delaware State to pursue a Bachelor's and Master's in Criminal Justice. Debra wants to be a juvenile advocate, and to one day own and manage her own group home for young women. She lives by two scriptures, Philippines 4:13 and Isaiah 54:17.

Corvid

Artist: Graham Alston

Graham Alston is a student at Chesapeake College, but he also
works in the College's bookstore. He's majoring in the
biological sciences. In his free time, he enjoys sketching and
writing short fiction.

Hurt
by Rebekkah Napier

I am the fighter who defends you from home.
In the darkest of nights, I'll walk out alone.
I'll fight for your kind, my kind (the same).
I'll die for you who don't care for my name.
I've given you all and ask you for none.
Still, you yell and threaten with the end of a gun.
I kept you safe, brought evil to justice,
and now you will thank me with anger and fists.

I am the warrior in lands unknown.
I earned your freedom, with you safely home.
Bullets and bombs – I faced them all.
I know what it's like to watch my friends fall.
Now, you scorn the flag that I've protected,
and think you're strong for all you've rejected?
I fear no fight, or did you forget?
You're just an athlete. I'm a battle-torn vet.

I am the voice of the bruised and oppressed.
You say I am lower, though this country's progressed.
For all your learning, you don't comprehend
this country's that's "free" is morally bent.
At home and at war we fought beside whites,
but still we're abused and denied equal rights.
They brought the chain, the whip, and the plow!
They say they brought freedom. Well, where is it now?!

We are the voices, loud and strong,
and we shall rage like a violent song!
For rage we will and rage we might!
Against our own side, we fiercely fight!

I am the voice to be left unsung,
as I watch my country be slowly undone.
Both sides want justice, to be rid of their dread,
but though they want new, they dredge up the dead!
It all could be bygones, left behind in the past,

but they nurture their pain and hold to it fast.
My heart has been torn. It has broken and shattered,
as I watch the dissolution of all that mattered!
This war divides a land united,
but what will it take for the wrong to be righted?
The sparring of words? The throwing of mud?
A battle that ends with a river of blood?

Yet here I remain, the voice unsung,
as I watch my home be forever undone.
You all strive to see the violence is quelled.
However, the enemy, in truth, is ourselves.
So many ask, "Who will join in the fray?"
But I ask you, "Why must you hurt me this way?"

Rebekkah Napier is a 19 year old, second year student at Chesapeake College. She grew up on the Eastern Shore and is proud to be a small town girl. Rebekkah inherited her creative genes from her mother and father. She and her sister enjoy crafting, creating anything, and writing. Her parents have always been supportive of her creative endeavors, and after college, Rebekkah hopes to make a living out of her creativity by writing novels or screenplays.

Fusion
Dedicated to Carlos Santana

Artist: Miriam Moran

Miriam Moran is a New York born, upcoming artist attending Chesapeake College. She has painted for well-known celebrities, such as Lil Kim, Zeola Gaye in honor of her brother, Marvin Gaye, Cambridge civil rights activist, Gloria Richardson and more. Miriam hopes to continually be known for the passion and style in her art, as well as stirring up soulful emotional connections through her pieces.

Home, Sweet Home

by Katondra Cherry

Since I was a child, Baltimore has always been home to me. I never thought I could live away from my family and friends. Nothing ever seemed unnatural to me during my years spent in Baltimore City. Sadly, it was normal for me to be walking down the street and see a woman being beaten up by her boyfriend, or even getting "banked", as us Baltimorians would call it, by a group of girls. I would keep right on walking and mind my business. Even the smell of gunpowder was as frequent to my nose, as smelling a chicken box from the Historic Lexington Market. Crazy right? Yeah, for most people that is, but for me not so much. It was perfectly normal.

I wondered what my life would be like if I moved away? If I could stop at a light without some young kid squirting some concoction of God knows what on my car just to make a buck? If I could walk down a clean street without seeing a huge rat? Maybe I could go somewhere in peace and not have some drug junkie harassing me saying, "Aye shorty, you got a dolla'?" I even wondered what the silence of no police sirens sounded like. It seems like everywhere I went in Baltimore, I would have to hold on extra tight to my pocketbook. No one wanted to live like that. I know I didn't, and although I often dreamed about it, I never really had enough courage to leave. Quite frankly, I was tired of the craziness.

On September 1, 2013 at 3:30 PM, I peered upon hundreds of anticipating guests as butterflies began to bombard the pit of my stomach. My father escorted me slowly down the long immaculate aisle of the St. Michaels Catholic Cathedral. He carefully wiped the beads of sweat dripping from my beautifully arched brow. As each step grew closer, the excitement intensified, because I was seconds away from being united in holy matrimony with the love of my life. Hearing him say the words "I do" would only be confirmation and seal the deal to the change that would soon take place in my life.

One hot summer afternoon in August of 2014, the stench of manure and funky farm animals offensively filled the air. As we drove down Route 50 in a U-haul truck, I was wondering to myself, "Why did I decide to move here again?" "PEEEEYEEWW, it stinks Mommy!" Ashlynn, who is my youngest daughter, shouted. I chuckled at her being a grossed-out kid, as she reminisced about the putrid smell of the Baltimore zoo.

"I don't think I'm gonna like it here!" Cherish, my oldest daughter, shouted. "Daddy, where are we going any ole way?" she added.

"Cambridge, Maryland!" Jason proudly stated.

"That's where you're from, right dad?" Ash asked inquisitively.

"Yup," he replied. I just sat in boredom and listened. It wasn't until I saw a crab shack that my eyes widened with some excitement. As we drove further down the road, I saw about five more. Being a Baltimorian, I wasn't used to seeing all the cornfields and greenery, but I started to think that since I was a lover of seafood, Cambridge would be quite alright with me.

Upon entering the driveway of our new single-family home, I could almost hear the children's heartbeats beating out of their chests with excitement. "Wooooooow" that's our house?" Ash asked.

"Yes, it is. Are you ready to go inside?" Before I could get a reply, they both were opening the front door. When I walked on the beautifully buffed hardwood floors, I couldn't believe my eyes. I was standing in my new home. It was so gorgeous and unlike anything I was used to. We had a real fireplace. When I turned it on and saw the fire, you could've bought me for a penny! We all were in such amazement by the fabulous attributes of the home. We even had stainless steel appliances. "Let's go pick our rooms," Ashlynn shouted. Before we scurried upstairs, we removed our shoes as we didn't want to stain the fluffy, cushioned beige carpet with our dirty, worn soles.

First, Ashlynn chose her room, as she was the youngest and it was a "no brainer" that Jason and I would have the master suite. "Mommy, I want this big room," Ash yelled with authority.

"Ok sweetie it's all yours," I replied. Cherish chose her room, and then we all came to see the main attraction, which was the master bedroom. My jaws literally dropped when I entered the double doors to my enormous bedroom. I had already passed by two bathrooms, but when I saw my personal bathroom, inside my bedroom, I almost fainted. I had a stand-up shower in my bathroom, not to mention his and hers sinks, and a Jacuzzi tub. My house, then, turned into a home.

After everyone chose their rooms and examined the house thoroughly, night fell. In Cambridge, nighttime is nothing like the busy, noisy streets of Baltimore. It was very dark and quiet, as there were no streetlights like the big city where I was from. It was so quiet, I could hear the crickets. The silence of the night frightened me and made it impossible for me to sleep. I was so accustomed to hearing the loud "BANG" of gunshots, ambulances, and police sirens at night. I curled up in bed next to my husband, and he cradled me as a mother would her newborn baby. He softly kissed me on the hollows of my cheek and whispered, "This is what peace feels like. Now, rest baby."

The next morning, we woke up all wanting different foods to eat. In Baltimore, I knew I could get a "chicken box" and "half and half" at any time of the day. "Jason, I want a chicken box," I said.

He replied, "Uhm? Baby this is Cambridge and we have wing dings and fries!" I laughed hysterically and said, "That sounds foolish, but it's the same thing." To my surprise, everything was closed on Sundays. I began to inquire about stores that sell the foods I like.

He told me in a sarcastic voice, "You better go to Food Lion." I thought to myself, "Did I move to North Carolina?" Everything was miles and miles away; there were no corner stores, delis, or bodegas. Everyone talks weird, people wave for no reason, and it stinks here. I was going to need some time to get used to this strange place.

Over the course of the next few months or so, I began to get used to life on the Eastern shore. My kids began school at Maple Elementary School, where my oldest daughter was the captain of the flag team, under the tutelage of Ray Washington. She has had the opportunity to perform for a televised halftime Baltimore Ravens game on their field, not to mention a plethora of other major opportunities she has been awarded while attending Maple. Although Ashlynn is too young to remember her short years spent in Baltimore, Cherish remembered hers quite well. She often told me how she's glad we moved to the Shore. Since we've lived here, she hasn't been in one physical altercation. Cherish tells me, "Mom I'm so glad I have my own bathroom and room now."

In conclusion, being a new resident of Cambridge is not about the luxurious home, or all the seafood my eyes can see, but more so about my children growing up in a safe, positive, more diverse, family-oriented environment that challenges them to make the right choices in life and utilize their people skills. Cambridge is now what we call, "Home Sweet Home".

Katondra Cherry-Jenkins, "Muff", is a professional singer and dental assistant. She's a native of Baltimore City and currently resides in Cambridge. Katondra is a wife and mother of two beautiful girls. She's a freshman at Chesapeake College and plans to transfer to UMES for Dental Hygiene. Katondra has traveled the world and has a passion for fashion. She believes you can obtain any goal you plan to achieve; success has no limitations.

Beach Day
by Marissa Moldoch

Foaming waves crashing on the sandy shore.
Ice cream melting; kids asking for more.
The sun beating down on the people so pale.
Boats gliding across the water with the wind in their sails.
Busy workers taking the time to relax.
Sunglasses, bathing suits, and floppy hats.
Delicate little castles created with care.
Abundant picnic lunches with food to spare.
Seashells of various shapes and sizes.
A sparkling tide that falls and rises.
Think it all sounds too good to be true?
Wait another minute, and I'll give you a clue.
It's not far away; it's within arm's reach,
Since this is what you'll see on your day at the beach.

Six Sisters
by Jacky Smith

*Interior of dining room. Walls are sponge painted a robin's egg blue
color. A pearly flowery border wraps the room at chair rail height. Below
the border, the wall is solid robin's egg blue. On the back wall there is a
large picture window overlooking a forest and lake. Two chairs that
match the dining set flank the windows. To the right there is a swinging
door to the kitchen. On the same wall, there is a sideboard filled with
dishes and two drink pitchers with a stack of glasses. To the left is an open
archway to the living room. On the same wall, a buffet stands with a
cabinet atop with glass doors full of china and delicate mementos. The
center of the room is occupied by a large, oblong dining room table. That
is surrounded by 6 chairs. An empty napkin holder, ashtray, and salt and
pepper set sit on the table.*

Characters:

Kathy- A tall, sturdily built dark haired 45-year-old woman. She would be
described as a handsome woman.

Jenny- A thin dark-haired girl about the age of 13. She's always in motion,
whether it's her foot tapping, or her hands fidgeting.

Sue- She is obese, shorter than Kathy, and 47 years old. She perpetually
smokes. Her dyed hair is growing out and gray roots are obvious.

Carm- A a slim 52-year-old. Her hair is perfectly coiffed bubble of vague
beige-y hair, and she is very made up. She is the epitome of mom-ness in
her clothes with her high-waisted jeans and blousy top.

Brenda- She is too-thin and dressed slightly too young for her age of 54.
Her hair is over-processed brunette. She's all angles, nothing soft about
her; think Maleficent in street clothes.

June- She is 43, closest in height to Kathy, with yellow-blonde hair. She
dresses as if it's still the 70s, in her satin top with a vest and faded jeans.
There's a detachment to her demeanor, nothing seems to really get to her.

Carole- Is the oldest at 60 and dresses like a catalog model, very on trend. Her hair is platinum blonde and perfectly styled. She could have fallen out of a sitcom show (Growing Pains, perhaps), appearances are clearly important to her.

*****

Kathy enters, looking harried. She's followed by a lanky, younger version of herself, her daughter Jenny. The woman carries serving spoons and places them on the sideboard to the right, setting them carefully with the dishes on the sideboard. The daughter carries napkins and places them into a napkin holder on the table. As soon as she's finished and moves away, the mother steps over and adjusts them.

Kathy: Go make sure the boys haven't left toys in the entryway. They should be here any minute.

Jenny: Okay. *(Jenny exits through archway.)*

Kathy: *(To herself.)* Okay, okay, I think that's everything. *(Smooths her outfit nervously.)*

Jenny: *(Calls from other room.)* Auntie Sue is here!

Kathy: *(Calls back.)* Okay, show her in*! (To herself.)* Shit! The ice! *(She leaves through the swinging door.)*

(Muffled sounds of greetings from the other room. Jenny shows Sue into the room.)

Jenny: Mom made lunch. *(She gestures to the buffet, then pauses, remembers herself.)* Can I get you a drink? We have iced tea and water.

Sue: Does your mom have any pop?

Jenny: Um, let me check. *(She exits through the swinging door. Sue pulls a cigarette case from her pocket and lights up. She wanders around the room, looking at everything. Kathy enters.)*

Kathy: Hey Sue, I have some Pepsi.

Sue: Diet?

Kathy: No, I'm sorry. *(Jenny enters behind her.)*

Jenny: Should I bring out the pop?

Sue: No, I guess tea will be fine.

Kathy: Jenny, you didn't take Auntie Sue's coat! *(Kathy moves to get a drink for Sue.)*

Jenny: *(Sighs.)* I'm sorry, I was trying to get her a drink.

Sue: It's fine. *(She takes off her coat and hands it to Jenny, who disappears to the other room.)*

Jenny: *(Calls from other room.)* Auntie Carm and Auntie Brenda are here! *(More muffled greetings, this time Jenny ushers in Carm and Brenda and immediately holds out her arms.)* Can I take your coats, please? *(Carm and Brenda surrender their coats, and Jenny leaves with them through arched doorway.)*

Kathy: Can I get you something to drink? *(She hands Sue her tea.)* There's tea, and lemonade-

Brenda: Do you have coffee?

Kathy: I can make some.

Brenda: Oh good, I was worried when I didn't smell any.

Carm: I'll have coffee too.

Jenny: I can make it, Mom.

Kathy: *(Shakes her head.)* No, that's okay, I got it. *(Kathy and Jenny move out of the room through the swinging door, moments later Jenny returns, looking glum, she seats herself by the window in one of the chairs. She looks at her hands.)*

Carm: Well Kathy certainly went to a lot of trouble. *(She moves to sideboard.)* Look at all this food!

Brenda: I'm looking at the walls. *(Jenny's attention perks up, she's listening.)*

Sue: Can't help but look at them.

Carm: It's certainly creative.

Sue: I guess.

Kathy: *(Kathy calls from kitchen.)* Jenny, Auntie June is here, go let her in! *(Jenny gets to her feet and moves through the archway. She returns a moment later with June. She exits with June's coat, and returns to take her seat, then remembers.)*

Jenny: Auntie June, would you like a drink?

June: Sure, what do you have?

Jenny: We have iced tea, water, Pepsi, and coffee.

June: Iced tea sounds good. *(Jenny moves to get her drink.)*

Kathy: There you are! I was worrying about you, I thought you said you'd be by an hour ago.

June: The asshole didn't pick up the kids until 11, so I came as soon as I could. How's it going?

Kathy: Haven't really gotten started yet. Get some food ladies, while we wait for Carole.

Sue: *(Chuckles.)* She'll be late to her own funeral.

Brenda: I'm sure something came up.

June: Then something always comes up. She's always late.

(The sisters fix themselves plates. Kathy exits swinging door to kitchen to fetch another serving spoon.)

Brenda: *(Picks something up and examines it.)* What the hell is this?

Jenny: *(From her chair)* It's a cucumber sandwich.

Brenda: *(Nods absentmindedly at Jenny, then mutters to Carm at her side.)* Don't sandwiches usually have two pieces of bread?

Jenny: *(Defiantly.)* It's an OPEN-FACED cucumber sandwich. *(Brenda turns to face her as Kathy enters. She immediately picks up on the vibe, sees the anger on her daughter's face, turns to see agitation on Brenda's face.)*

Kathy: *(Concerned.)* Do we have everything we need?

Carm: Everything is fine. *(She nudges Brenda, who goes back to filling her plate.)*

(The women seat themselves at the table. Kathy sits near the center, June to her right. The other sisters sit on the other side of Kathy. One seat is left open for Carole at the left.)

Sue: So what ideas do we have for Mom's birthday?

Brenda: We should wait for Carole.

June: If we wait for Carole we might miss Mom's birthday. *(Sue, Kathy, and Carm laugh.)*

Brenda: Kathy, we were noticing what you've done with the walls in here.

Kathy: *(Noting that this is not necessarily a compliment, a little defensively.)* I saw it in a magazine. I wanted to try it.

June: I like it. It's colorful and interesting, not like my boring off-white walls. Stupid rental.

Kathy: Thanks!

Sue: You'll have to cover it when you move, won't you?

Carm: *(Before Kathy can respond, Carm jumps in.)* So, what was your idea, Kathy?

Kathy: I was thinking that we could do something for Mom that she can't do for herself any more. It's so frustrating for her, to be surrounded by reminders of things she can't do. She has all those flower beds, and they were mostly empty last year. What if we all chipped in and got some miracle grow and flowers and bulbs? It wouldn't be too expensive. We could all get together and redo those beds. It wouldn't take long if we all pitched in together. We could knock it out in a weekend. A family project. A sister project. Then mom could look at them and enjoy them all year. She'd love to look at it and know that maybe the petunias are from Sue, and the alyssum are from me, and the tulips are from June-

Brenda: We get the idea.

Kathy: We could each pick our favorite flowers.

Carm: It does sound thoughtful.

(A small noise is heard offstage.)

Brenda: I think Carole is here. *(She smiles, while Kathy's hopeful smile disappears.)*

(Kathy nods to Jenny, and Jenny moves through the archway to go greet Carole. Murmured greetings and Jenny and Carole enter room.)

Jenny: Can I get you a drink, Auntie Carole?

Carole: No, I'm fine.

Kathy: Would you like me to fix you a plate?

Carole: No, I ate on the way.

Kathy: Oh... I thought I told you I was making lunch.

Carole: Mm hm, I was starving.

June: If you had been on time, you wouldn't have been so hungry.

Carole: I just had so much to do before I could leave. It's tough with three boys.

Brenda: Even with two, it's tough.

Kathy: I have three and a daughter, I know what you mean.

Carole: Yes, but you were already here. It's not as if you could have been late. *(a moment of pause)*

Kathy: Are you sure I can't get you a drink?

Carole: I guess I could take some coffee, if you've made any. I wouldn't want to be a bother.

Kathy: Okay.

(Kathy leaves the room through swinging door to get the coffee. Carole takes Kathy's seat. June stares at her.)

Carole: So, what did I miss?

Brenda: Kathy has an *idea. (She says idea in a very condescending manner.)*

June: I liked the idea. *(She looks to Carm and Sue, who remain impassive.)*

Kathy: *(Returns with the coffee, sees Carole in her seat, pauses for just a beat, then moves to bring Carole the coffee.)* Here you go. *(She sits in the unoccupied chair at the end of the table.)*

Carole: So, what's this idea, Kathy?

Kathy: Well, I was thinking-

Carole: *(Sips coffee.)* Mmhmm?

Kathy: I was thinking that we could do something nice for mom.

Carole: Well, that would be the thing to do on her birthday. *(She laughs.)*

Kathy: Mom has all those empty flower beds-

Carole: *(Interrupts)* Well, it's not like she can take care of them.

Kathy: Exactly. And I know it bothers her to see them empty. So, I was thinking-

Sue: *(Quietly.)* You said that.

Kathy: -that we'd redo them for her. Then she could enjoy the flowers. And she'd be so happy that we all worked together on that.

Carole: *(Spoken as if to a child)* That's a sweet idea.

Brenda: I don't think I'd have the time to spend a weekend tearing up all those flower beds. I work two jobs.

June: I have time. And I could get the kids to help.

Sue: *(Thinking aloud.)* Ugh, that's so frustrating though, trying to get any work done while the kids run around. You'd end up spending more time minding the kids than working on the project.

Kathy: Jenny could watch the younger ones, she could walk them to the park. *(Jenny nods in the background.)*

Carole: I just don't know. With my boys' schedules, it's really hard to find time. I can only stay for a little bit today because I have to go pick Brian up and drop Chris off at his friend's. I was thinking we'd all chip in on a fancy lunch. Someplace nice, someplace mom wouldn't spend the money on herself to go.

June: Mom doesn't like "fancy". Mom likes simple and good. *(Kathy nods.)*

Brenda: *(Scathingly.)* I hardly think we're going to find a restaurant that serves chili mac or rice and beans.

Carole: I just picture Mother telling Anna or one of her other friends, "The girls got me dirt and flowers for my birthday". I mean, this is a big birthday. You don't turn 75 every day.

Kathy: But-

Carm: What restaurants did you have in mind?

Carole: What about Via Roma? Or La Francais?

June: Mom won't be able to eat half the stuff at those places.

Brenda: Which still leaves half the menu that she CAN eat.

Sue: True.

Kathy: *(Quietly.)* They sound expensive.

Carole: Not really, we pay for ourselves and our families, and then split mom's meal. It's not really that expensive at all.

Brenda: I think it'd be nice, instead of her cooking for a change.

June: And you only have to pay for you, since your boys are out of state. Some of us have to pay for four kids, our husbands, and ourselves.

Brenda: Well at least you have Rick to pay for it for you. I don't have anyone, I have to pay my own way.

June: *(Angrily.)* Trust me, I pay plenty.

Carole: It's really not any more expensive that a family dinner out.

Kathy: I don't usually take the kids to La Francais. And both of those restaurants are really far south. Couldn't we go somewhere closer to mom?

Carole: You mean, closer to you?

Kathy: Because I live by mom.

Carole: It's not my fault that Steve's work brought us closer to the city.

Kathy: Of course not. I never said it was.

Carole: Well I was only suggesting restaurants that are nice that *I* know of. What are some good restaurants in this area? *(Kathy opens her mouth, but Carole cuts her off.)* Carm? What's good up here?

Carm: Well, there's Tsukasa, and Gale Street Inn. It's a shame Journey's End closed, she liked that place.

June: Or Dover Straits.

Sue: I got food poisoning the last time I ate there.

June: Wasn't when I worked there.

Sue: Did I say it was?

Kathy: *(Trying again.)* So, no one even wants to consider the garden idea?

Carole: I just don't want to give my mother dirt on her 75th birthday.

(Kathy rises and moves to the sideboard to start putting away the food that's barely been touched. Her head hangs a little. She knows she's been defeated.)

June: Yeah, why give her dirt that she can keep when we can give her a meal that she'll just crap out a few hours later?

(Kathy smiles at the sideboard but conceals it from her sisters, Jenny laughs aloud, and the other sisters look appalled. June is looking at Kathy's back, she knows she's smiling.)

Sue: June!

(June shrugs and smiles, their disdain amuses her.)

Kathy: Does anyone want anything else? I'm going to start clearing up. I wouldn't want to hold Carole's boys' social plans up.

Carole: I think Mom is really going to like her lunch. Carm, get me a list of restaurants and I'll call around to see who will take reservations.

(She rises to her feet and Sue and Brenda follow suit. Carm has a piece of food halfway to her mouth but sets it on her plate and pushes her chair back. A phone rings in the background. Jenny bounds out of the room to answer it.)

Jenny: *(Calls from other room.)* AUNTIE JUNE!

June: Shit, I bet that's the asshole. Never should have told him what my plans were. *(She moves through swinging door into kitchen.)*

Carole: Thank you for getting us all together, Kathy. This was nice. I love what you've done with this room. *(She smiles.)* It's so... different!

(Jenny comes back into room.)

Sue: *(Sharply to Jenny.)* So do we get our coats back? *(She's smiling but it's not a real smile.)*

Jenny: *(A little haughty.)* Of course. *(She leaves room through arch to gather coats.)*

Brenda: *(Rolls eyes.)* That one is going to be trouble.

Carole: It only seems that way to us, Bren, we don't have girls. Thank you, Kathy, for getting us all together. This was nice.

Brenda: *(Smiling like the cat who ate the canary.)* Wasn't it?

June: *(Reenters room. Exasperated.)* I have to go. Jessie is barfing. And of course, he refuses to handle it. *(Quietly to Kathy.)* I'm sorry.

(They kiss Kathy on the cheek, one by one, quick pecks. Jenny enters carrying the coats in one big armload.)

Carole: Oh, be careful with my fur.

Jenny: *(Slightly insincere.)* Oh, sorry. *(She carelessly drops the coat into Carole's hands.)*

Kathy: I'm glad mine's faux, I don't have to worry about it so much.

Carole: That must be nice to not have to worry about something so valuable.

(The women move through the archway, Kathy following behind.)

Kathy: Thanks for coming.

(Jenny moves to sideboard and fixes herself a very full plate as goodbyes are said in the next room. She almost sits in the chair Carole just vacated, then changes her mind and sits in the chair that Kathy was sitting in. Kathy comes back in and gets herself a glass of lemonade. She sits in her original seat and lights a cigarette.)

Jenny: *(Matter-of-factly.)* I hate them. *(Takes a bite of food, speaks with mouth full.)* Well, Auntie June's okay.

Kathy: Don't talk with your mouth full. *(Pause.)* You shouldn't say that.

Jenny: You should hate them too. They're mean.

Kathy: They're...they're my sisters.

Jenny: So?

Kathy: *(Shakes her head.)* You don't understand. You have brothers.

Jenny: I'm glad! *(They're quiet for a moment.)* We're gonna still do the garden, right?

Kathy: *(Pauses.)* Yes, I think we will. *(She puffs on her cigarette.)*

Jenny: It's a good idea, Mom. *(She looks at her mother's face, concerned.)*

Kathy: *(Smiles briefly, then sighs.)* So, what did they say when I was out of the room?

CURTAIN

THE BEACON IS NOW ACCEPTING SUBMISSIONS

thebeaconatchesapeake.wordpress.com
theccbeacon@gmail.com

- POETRY - PROSE - FICTION - SHORT PLAYS -
SCRIPTS- ESSAYS - ARTWORK - PHOTOGRAPHY -